How To Analyze People Conversation Tactics

The Best Strategies for Successful Conversations and Negotiations for Beginners

Kevin Bradnik

ISBN-13: 978-1544234670
ISBN-10: 1544234678

FOREWORD

I want to thank you and congratulate you for buying Conversation Tactics: The Best Strategies for Successful Conversations and Negotiations for Beginners.

Communication is a key skill that is required to progress through the ranks in corporate America. You need to feel confident in your abilities to communicate complex ideas in a variety of situations. I aim to provide you with strategies and tips to negotiate your salary, make a presentation, make a major sale or purchase, and even help you improve your small talk to get better at networking with your colleagues and new faces. The truth of the matter is that these skills are paramount to having the best possible experience in the workplace. In our modern age of constant communication through electronic devices, many have found it more difficult than ever to have serious face-to-face communications between fellow workers and superiors. The good news is there are strategies that you can invoke to have the best possible experience in these different situations.

I decided to write this book because my field of work and research in the study of executive compensation. What I have found is that part of the reason why executive compensation has ballooned in the last twenty years has to do with the increased amount of information executives find about each other's salaries. In addition, they have skills that benefit them in their high-level corporate roles. These skills are not inherent; the lucky ones were not born with them. These are learnable skills, however, that allow for better presentations and negotiation ability--skills you will need in corporate America.

By reading this book, you will come away with the key pieces of knowledge you need to improve your communication skills in all aspects of the corporate world. If you do not develop these skills, you will forever struggle to get what you want from your coworkers and superiors. Negotiations require practice and skill, but above all they require the knowledge to work through these difficult situations effectively. This is a small investment in your future, but one that will pay dividends in ways that you have never imagined. You can have a bigger salary, make greater connections at work, and improve your ability to buy and sell products for your company and home. In addition, the invaluable skill of small talk will help you network with other professionals in your field, opening the door to limitless opportunities as you expand your reach in your profession.

You don't need to be afraid of making requests to upper management or your boss; you don't need to be fearful of making presentations both large and small. Start reading and invoking the tips and strategies I offer and you will find that you are better positioned to become a better earner for you and your family. You will have the confidence to speak with authority and gain the salary and respect you deserve. Simply continue reading and where you can go in the professional world will expand to new heights.

Kevin Bradnik

Contents

CHAPTER 1: SALARY NEGOTIATIONS

Empathy and Perspective

The first component of a successful negotiation of your salary is to put yourself in the shoes of your superior. From the research I have done, I have found it quite common that there is a slight sense of resentment that builds up in those who are planning on asking for an increase in compensation. This comes from the employee thinking about all the good they have done for their employer and viewing a compensation increase from the perspective that they absolutely deserve to be paid more. While the issue of whether or not it is is deserved does not change, the problem is that this line of thinking leads down a path of negativity. Therefore, the first aspect of planning your negotiation is to put yourself in the shoes of your boss, or whoever will ultimately be making the decision on your compensation. This should not change how you plan on illustrating all of the good that you have done for your employer, but it does help diffuse any resentment that might be building up. I am keen on this being the first point on which to focus because with feelings of negativity, aspects of what you have done in your current role often get overlooked. You must keep a good record of your actions and go into a meeting with the best possible attitude. Build your argument from this vantage point: what can I present that will persuade them, instead of thinking about what you have already done to earn that increase in compensation.

Timing

After you have put yourself in the position of your boss in order to build your argument why you should get an increase in compensation, it is time to think about the planning the timing of your salary negotiation. If you are applying for a position at a new company, it is difficult to have your job history on your side. If you are planning for an increase in compensation at your current job, however, then you must absolutely make this work to your advantage. Make an appointment for a meeting with your superior on a Thursday or Friday, and do so when the workload at the place of your employment is low to average. If your salary negotiation is for a new job, you may find that the timing is out of your control; but when presented with an option, you always want to shoot for later in the week.

It is a simple tip, but it can make all the difference in the world. You will want to enter into a salary negotiation on a Thursday or Friday because your boss wants to clear away their worries and lingering tasks before the end of the week. It has been shown through studies I have conducted, as well as past studies by other researchers, that employers are more likely to grant compensation increases right before the weekend. The logic behind this has to do with clearing away all their present tasks before the end of the week, but it has to do with even more than this. It is the time when people around the office are likely to be in the best possible mood. Act on this and you will find that your request has increased odds of success by merely changing the timing of your request.

You do not want to go into a salary negotiation when the office is most hectic. The reason for this is simple; your boss is going to have far more on his or her mind during times when the office is busy and you will be subject to their emotions about how busy it is. You want your superior to be in the best possible mood and to have full focus on what you are bringing to their attention. Therefore, zero in on bringing your salary negotiation to your boss when the workload is low to average so that you can make your case and have their undivided attention.

Speak to Recruiters at Other Companies

Researching compensation at your current company is similar to looking for a new job. You will want to talk to job recruiters and get an idea of what people with your title currently get paid. This is a tricky maneuver as you don't want to make it clear to your current employer that you are looking for a new job. As such, you will need to be discreet and focus on this type of research at home. This is easy if you are negotiating for a new job, but it will be more laborious if you are already employed. Know that the work you have to do outside of the office will always be worth the increase in your compensation.

You also need to make sure that you are fair with the job recruiters to whom you are speaking. It is an extremely common tactic to look at competing companies to increase your compensation at your current company, or at the company where you have made the most progress towards employment. The best way to be fair, but also glean the information you need from recruiters, is to go along with interviews requests for information up to the point of filling out any official government forms. This is a good dividing line between getting the information you want and not being sensitive to the job responsibilities of those from whom you getting information. There is another way to get this information fairly and that is simply to befriend the job recruiter. This requires that you have a good relationship with the person with whom you are communicating; but it is fruitful if you can be straight forward and tell them that you are looking at offers from competing companies.

Lastly, although you likely have your first choice of the business for whom you want to work, whether it is your current company or the one you are furthest along with in terms of interviews, you should always consider the offers of competing companies. Moving along with recruiters and gaining information on compensation and job responsibilities is a good way to test the waters of what it would be like to work for someone else. You must consider the possibility that the best fit is not where you currently work, nor your current first choice for a company. It might simply be that your best choice is actually an organization that you have not considered in the past. Along these lines, don't worry about loyalty to an organization beyond the point that it matters what your overall compensation will be. You owe something your employer or the person with whom you have made the most inroads, only to the extent that they return your trust. If they are unwilling to budge on negotiations, or are severely low-balling compensation figures, it might be time to consider taking a recruiter up on their offer and testing what it would be like to work for a different company.

Research Compensation at Competing Companies

Whether you are re-negotiating your current salary or negotiating for a brand new job, you need to be aware of what other employees in your position or a similar role are being paid. *GlassDoor.com* is excellent tool to do exactly this, but even this amazing resource will only help you so much. The problem is that there is a lack of clarity between a job role and a job title. For example, the duties that you take on under your job title may be far different from what you find in competing companies. You may find that you have far more responsibilities but are given a lower paying job title; this happens all the time. There are a few ways to get past this problem and all of them involve some research.

This research will be your greatest tool in maximizing your compensation. Executive compensation has greatly increased in the last twenty years. The great increase in executive compensation has come about because executives now have more information about what their peers are making. This information is available to you for your job role, too; you just have to look hard enough to find it. What you should be looking for are jobs that match your level of responsibility. For new hires, this means taking a look at job responsibilities as outlined during your interview with a new company. You can then take these responsibilities and match them to online data for similar jobs. Employees looking for greater pay can also do the same. This type of research is best done through a simple command on Google and limiting the search for data within *GlassDoor.com*. The command you want to use is:

Description of your current job responsibilities, **site:glassdoor.com**

This limits all of your searches to *GlassDoor.com* so that you can find jobs with a different title but that have the same responsibilities for the job for which you are applying, or currently have. This will get you beyond the tricky aspect of finding the current compensation for jobs that have the same description but end up having different job titles overall. This is not information that you need to bring in with you, but rather it should be in the calculation of what you plan on asking from your employer. Remember that you will need to have a firm idea of what you are seeking before you walk into any negotiations. This number needs to be based on real and present data; you will never need to actually present this data however. Trust me when I say that the person you are negotiating with knows the true value of what your job is worth in the outside market. Besides, you will also have the data from job recruiters that will give you definite figures as to the appropriate salary.

There is one last aspect to researching what your compensation would be at a different company online, and this is the cost of living where you live. Thirty thousand dollars in Kansas is far different from thirty thousand dollars in New York City. Make sure that you are paying attention to from where workers are reporting their salaries. You have to adjust for the cost of living in different places. There are a few calculations that will allow you to this, but I have found that the best research papers for normalizing the cost of living do so based on rent and purchased housing; the other costs of daily living are insignificant enough that they don't matter nearly as much as the cost of housing. You will want to look at what rent or the cost of buying a house is in the city where you are obtaining figures for compensation. In addition, you will want to pay attention to the taxes in the given state. It is difficult to make an argument for higher pay due to taxes; this is entirely out of the hands of your employer, but you will want to be aware of the tax rate in certain states. For example, New Jersey is notorious for high taxes for commuters who travel in from New York. Again, you really can't use this as an argument for higher pay, but it can influence your decision as to the firm you want to work for. In the case of New Jersey, it is often cheaper to work *and* live there than to commute from New York state.

An Argument for Yourself

Whether you are negotiating your salary for a new job or are negotiating a new salary for your existing job, you will want to create a single document that indicates all of your accomplishments. When applying for a new job, you should have handed in a résumé specific to the position desired. This is *not* the same piece of paper that you should be using when you are negotiating your salary. You should have gone through a few interviews with the company for which you will be working. During these interviews, you gleaned more information than you had when you first applied; use this information to tweak your résumé and gear it towards the exact position you will be filling. One suggestion when making this new document is to greatly change the style of it. Make it distinct from your résumé, even though a lot of the information will be shared. It is all too easy to present a document during negotiations but the individual may say that they already have your résumé on file. You really want to drive home that this is a different sheet of paper that justifies the salary for which you are asking.

If you are seeking increased compensation at the company for which you already work, you must create a new document that shows all that you have accomplished to date, specifically at your current job. This should be formatted much the same as your existing résumé. The important aspect of this document is to show the *results* of what you have accomplished. Make sure that these are indisputably your contributions to the company and that your superior cannot break down what you have claimed as only belonging partially to what you have contributed. If you work in a group, make your document focus on what you contributed to it and link it directly to the result. This is a great way to diffuse one of the most common counter tactics, arguing why other members of your team shouldn't also get a raise. You can push this issue aside by highlighting your own contributions and illustrating that you are sitting in your boss' office not for the good of the rest of your team, but because of what you specifically have accomplished.

Knowing What You Want but Letting Management Speak First

You've done the research and you've built yourself a document with all of your accomplishments listed at your current job. It is now time for the actual negotiations. When you go in, there is one last piece of information you need to prepare--what are you seeking as an increase in compensation. It is worth noting that not all forms of increased compensation come directly from salary. It is quite possible that what will be the most beneficial to you, and possibly to your employer, is an increase in others types of compensation. This includes things like a company car, a better parking spot, a new or larger office, increased retirement contributions, stock options, healthcare benefits and more paid vacation. The point is there is a lot that can happen during these negotiations, and you have to keep in mind that not all forms of increased compensation come from a direct increase in your pay.

When you go into negotiations, have three firm numbers in mind in terms of the salary you are trying to negotiate. You should also have a list of other perks that would be acceptable to you, possibly in addition to an increase in your base pay. The three numbers should represent the different outcomes that you would find acceptable, so there is a low number, a mid-range and an upper end/best result. Factor in other forms of compensation you might receive; and after you have explained what you are looking for, let your employer be the first to lay down the initial offer. You should *never* accept the first offer, and at a bare minimum seek to increase your form of compensation above your base pay. In most medium to large businesses, you can expect your employer to offer a combination of a wage hike and an increase in benefits. Pin this initial offer in your mind and see where it fits between the three numbers that you came up with. Now it is time to use this information in combination with your employer's initial offer to renegotiate your final compensation.

Your employer's offer is likely going to be between the upper end and the lower end of what you are willing to accept. The litmus test is going to be where it sits relative to the middle number that you have decided. You should use this to judge how forceful you are going to be about receiving greater compensation. These numbers should have been based off what professionals in the same line of work receive for compensation, but none of this data will have included certain types of benefits. If management's offer sits between the low figure and the mid- range number, you should make a counteroffer to bring your base pay up to the middle number you have selected *and* some form of other compensation. The safe road to take for additional compensation is more paid vacation. If management gives a figure in-between your mid-range and the high number, then you should only counter with either increased benefits or try to get the base pay up to the highest figure.

There are a lot of different outcomes possible here, including your employer trying to offer a number below your absolute lowest base pay increase. If this happens, don't fret, but it is a signal that you need to more clearly explain why you need the increase in pay. This is the *only* time where you should start considering stating what other recruiters are offering for the same type of job responsibilities. It's important that at a bare minimum you are hitting your lowest acceptable offer, and mentioning what other recruiters are willing to pay is sort of the nuclear option in salary negotiations. The reason this is such a potentially dangerous play is that it truly does threaten the company for which you currently work, or from whom you have just received an initial job offer. There is the possibility that the situation turns into a conversation about you leaving the company and going to work for the company that sponsors the recruiter to whom you have spoken. This is something you need to be prepared for; if you are going to negotiate and your boss is not willing to budge on the base salary you truly think you deserve, you might have to walk away from your current place of employment. Again, this all based around the idea that you have done the research and have spoken to the job recruiters interested in hiring you.

What If Management Says "No"

There is an additional possibility when negotiating for a higher salary that management might simply say "no." What matters in this scenario is *how* management refuses your request. Is it a matter of timing for the company and if so, are they willing to approach this subject again in the future? In this case, you want a timeline for when you can come to your boss again and talk about compensation. There is also the strong possibility, depending on the organization, that your boss says he or she has to talk to his or her superiors to get approval for any sort of increase in compensation. You should prepare yourself for the same type of response, trying to obtain when you can approach this subject again in the future. Do not be alarmed if this is the initial path that your salary negotiations take. There are many top-down run organizations that will have difficulty in increasing compensation for employees directly through a boss or supervisor.

It is important that if this is the initial wall you hit, you don't start making your case to your superior but first find out if a negotiation is on the table at all. You do not want to be in the position where you are negotiating for an increase in your salary multiple times. Every time you make an argument why you deserve an increase to compensation, it loses its effectiveness. You want to be able to make your argument once and make that argument to the person or people who have an immediate effect on your compensation.

CHAPTER 2: PRESENTATIONS

Many fields in corporate America rely on presentations to communicate information from one branch of a company to another. This can come in the form of a product presentation, but it also may come into play as part of simply explaining to other sections of the company what you and your team are working on and how your project will impact the rest of the company. Presentations are a great opportunity to show your worth to the company as a whole and to demonstrate the value that you add to the organization. The first aspect of creating the perfect presentation is to know exactly what you want to communicate.

Outlining Your Goals

The most important aspect of your product presentation is to let others understand that you are privy to knowledge that your audience simply isn't. You have spent a lot of time thinking about the project in question and are intimately familiar with the details. As such, you need to break away from your current way of thinking and start to view your project as something foreign, to take a step back from it and put yourself in the position of taking a new look at what you hope to explain. The best way to do this is to outline exactly what you want the audience to take away from your presentation.

To make this outline as efficiently as possible, and to explain clearly to your audience members the most important aspects of your presentation, you will want to create a list of questions you hope your audience can answer at the end. These questions will be your guide as to how to format your presentation and the information that is the most important or difficult to explain. Remember that there is more information than just what you are presenting; you have to keep in mind that there is probably some level of base knowledge needed to fully explain what you are trying to cover. Make sure that if your audience does not already have some base knowledge that it is included in the first part of your presentation. For example, if you are doing a presentation on a plan set in place to optimize any aspect of the business, be sure all members of the audience understand the inefficiencies that are currently in place. You need to make sure that they understand the need for what you are trying to solve, and the best way to do this is to illustrate the problem as clearly as possible.

This logic of attempting to give the audience an answer to a question they might not have is important in all presentations. Whether you are presenting a concrete product or are simply explaining a strategy that the company will be focusing on in the future, you must make sure that the *need* is well known to your audience. You have to present a problem as your initial first step and then spend the rest of your presentation trying to solve that problem with the work that you and your team have been focusing on. Focusing on this initial need is going to set the stage for why you are making a presentation in the first place. More importantly, it builds a narrative for your audience to follow that has a satisfying conclusion as you solve the problem or outline the strategies the company is going to take to reduce the complications of whatever you are trying to solve.

Tips for Building a Narrative for Your presentation

A narrative will hold the attention of your audience far longer than the details of your presentation. As an example, let's work on something that is specific and something that is dry: coffee sales for a fictional company. In this example, we need to make a presentation about how to improve coffee sales for a nationwide store. Beyond the initial impression that might gain some interest, this topic and minutia of it are extremely dry. The types of improvements that can be made in coffee sales rely on giving the sales staff new data and improving data collection on the types of coffee that people prefer. Let's suppose that the ultimate goal of this presentation is really simple: to explain two ways in which coffee shops can modify the way they handle sales to improve productivity and increase overall sales numbers.

Without a narrative to tie together the goals we wish to express for individual coffee stores, information disseminated to the audience will quickly filter out. The key to any narrative is that it has an arc, or a beginning, middle and end; with these details an audience is sure to remember the grand idea and the small details that make up the presentation. For this fictional presentation, suppose that the two measures to improve coffee sales are: one, to provide a discount card to customers where every fifth coffee purchase provides one free coffee, and two, a specialty coffee brew each week. To build a narrative from these two goals, we can focus on an individual family or a customer who has a relationship with the coffee chain. The changes the coffee store adopts could be reflected in the eyes of the consumers in our presentation. It is not that the presentation is dryly stating the changes in the business, but rather that the customer is describing the changes they witness. This creates an emotional bond with the audience; and even though we are presenting a fictional customer, they can relate to this person and see how their experience builds with the coffee store.

We have created our principle characters and how they relate to the store but have not truly crafted the arc that we need for our presentation. To do this, we simply have to focus on the character we have created and build a through line for their experiences with our coffee store. This narrative starts with the consumer having multiple options for where to buy coffee and that they like the specialty brews offered by other premium coffee stores. The middle of the arc details how the customer comes back to our stores because of the increased value of offering a discount card that gives the customer a reward for every fifth coffee. Finally, we establish a long-term connection that the customer will have with the store as the additional need of different types of coffee beans each week are served. We have successfully offered the same service as competing coffee stores, but have also added an additional benefit of a coffee rewards program. The audience is not only likely to remember the details of the presentation more clearly, which will surely also highlight expected growth in terms of percentage increases over the next few quarters, but they will also remember the changes suggested in the presentation more fondly. The emotional connection that we have formed between the audience and our fictional guest is sure to last long into the future.

CHAPTER 3: THE ART OF SALES

You Are Solving a Problem

It's easy to get caught up in the product or service you are trying to sell. You get entwined with it and know the inherent value it offers to customers. The problem with this deep-seated knowledge and appreciation is that it is completely absent from those to whom you are trying to sell. Much like making a presentation about a project you have completed, you need to build a narrative and explain the need for the product or service you are trying to sell.

The best way to start a sale is not to start with the product or service itself, but rather with the problem that it is trying to solve. To illustrate this, let's work with an example of a product that is one of the hardest to sell: knives. Knives are so hard to sell because everyone already has them. Whether it is standard cutlery or specialty cooking knives, this is a product that might seem impossible to move from inventory. The key is to explain the problem that currently exists in every household and how this problem can be solved with the product you are trying to sell. You are not a nuisance or a salesperson, but rather someone with answers to a problem you are illuminating.

In the example of selling knives, you need to have a common problem that you are trying to solve for customers.

Although they already have something that can accomplish the job of slicing and cutting, there are problems that cannot be solved with the current product they are using. You should mention these common problems like the tip of the knife falling off or knives needing sharpening after a number of years. Even if the product you are selling is not perfect, it has the attraction of being new. You can use this to solve any issue they might have with their current knives. Most importantly, you will spend your time illustrating the problem, magnifying it, and thus making your service necessary.

If you are trying to sell something that is not a good, but rather a service, the basic game plan does not change all that much. You are still trying to fix a fundamental problem for the customer. For example, let's focus on a service that fewer and fewer Americans are in need of each year: filling out their tax returns. This was once a service that many Americans would go to an accountant for, but nowadays they can do it themselves using relatively inexpensive software available on their home computers. You can still illustrate the value of this service by showing the common problems that can arise when tax returns are done incorrectly. You must simply focus on issues and how you can solve the customers' problems. Selling a tax service is one of the most difficult products because of the fact that many people believe they can handle the job themselves. If you can magnify the current problems of the customer, you will be in a better position to sell the tax service.

There is an important caveat to selling products by solving the problems of customer. You run the risk of being too negative, but this is something that can easily be mitigated by always moving on to solve the issue you are magnifying. It is not just that the knives they currently have do not cut well, but the knives that you are offering are actually going to fix this problem. It is not just that issues might arise from a customer doing their taxes by himself or herself, but rather that your service ensures the best possible outcome. If you always move on from the major problems you are trying to solve to immediately describing the solution, you will always create a positive atmosphere in which to sell your product.

The Price Always Comes Last

A good salesperson never mentions cost up front. You want to illustrate the uses of your product and why it is a necessity. You know that you are trying to solve a problem that exists for the customer and this needs to be demonstrated to the point that he or she begins to ignore the price. This is the battle you are always fighting; when a salesperson approaches, the customer immediately begins to thinks about the price of the good or service. If you can get that thought out of the customer's mind, then you have won them over. That is not to say that the cost of the product could make or break a sale, but if you can convince the customer for even a moment that they don't need to ask about price, then they are much more tempted to buy what you are selling.

Preparing an Elevator Pitch

There is a common strategy to sales that can be used to condense the selling points of your product or service. The strategy is to imagine all of your sales as taking place in an elevator. You and a customer walk into an elevator and you only have around thirty seconds to make your sales pitch. This is obviously not going to demonstrate all of the usefulness of the product you are trying to sell, but it does get you to think about the major selling points and create a description that can be given quickly. You have to find out what is the most interesting or captivating aspect of your product and then convey this to the customer in a short amount of time. Once you have grabbed their interest, it is the point when you fill in the details. If you can combine this aspect of sales with the advice from chapter six about presenting yourself to the customer, you will captivate and hold the attention of those to whom you are trying to sell for long enough to make the sale.

Chapter 4: Making a Purchasing Decision

Whether buying a product or service for personal use or making a purchasing decision on behalf of your company, buying can be just as stressful as making a sale. You have many objectives when buying a product: you are trying to determine if it will fit your needs, if there is a better product or service out there, and the whole time you must ultimately consider the cost. There are some strategies that you can follow to ultimately be content with any purchasing decision you make. All you have to do is ensure that you satisfy the following basic questions and you will be on your way to making an intelligent purchase that all concerned parties can be happy with.

Utility for You and a Nicety for the Seller

The first aspect in buying is to ensure that you are in need of the product you are considering. There are items that are superfluous and there are items that serve dedicated needs. Be realistic about whether or not the product you are looking at is going to fill the role that you need. Whether this item is for work or entertainment purposes, make an outline of the goals you want the product to serve. Make sure that you ask the salesperson about the good or service in enough detail that you are able to figure out if it meets all of your needs. You should phrase the questions that you have in a way such that they answer the essential question "Do I need this product?" This is the best way to determine what you are willing to pay for it, and if that product is a necessary purchase. This is easy enough to accomplish for goods that serve a utility, but for goods that fit the purpose of entertainment, you still have to outline the ultimate purpose that the product is trying to fill. The more objectives you can cross off your list as the item fulfills these roles, the better the purchasing decision you are going to make.

How you present yourself to the seller of these goods is very different from the cold calculations you make about the product filling the objectives you have. You must convey to the seller that there are many competing goods and services that can fill your request. This will get the seller to better illustrate the strong points of the product or service, but also puts him or her at a lower position in being able to sell. They won't be able to use the leverage of having a product that you need if you make it look like you do not require the product at all. By making it seem as though the product the seller is trying to convince you to buy is something that is a side purchase, then it will try much harder to make the sale. This may result in a reduction in price. The key to doing this in a way that shows you may still purchase the product and are staying at an advantage can be tricky. You need to show that you are once both interested in what they are trying to sell, but do not need to walk out the door having made a definite purchasing decision. You can do this by asking questions about the goods or service, being specific about what is on offer, but also by mentioning competing products and services you are looking at. This will cause the salesperson to mention the specialties that their product serves that other brands do not.

Shop Around

There is a golden rule to ensure that every purchase you make is one that you indeed *need*; wait a day after thinking about buying a product and if you still believe you need it, make the purchase. You should use this time to shop around for competing products or services that offer the same value. It also allows you to look up reviews and compare the different products and how they compete. The amount or research you do should be proportional to the cost of the product or service you are trying to obtain. Shopping for a house requires months of effort to make sure that you have considered all your options. When purchasing a lamp on the other hand, you can quickly look over your other options and then make a decision.

Bring in Other Offers

Shopping around and looking at competing goods and services is a great way to make a more informed purchasing decision, but you can also use the information and bring it back to the seller of the best version of the product or service, or the one that you are most inclined to buy, to reduce the cost. Be aware that many goods and services cannot be negotiated, but as purchases get more expensive, you have more wiggle room to obtain the ultimate cost. Goods that retail for less than one thousand dollars, for example, will have little wiggle room. It is unlikely that the sales staff can truly help you with the prices on these goods, but once purchases start to teeter over one thousand dollars, suddenly you will find that there is much more room to negotiate price.

The Hidden Costs

Always consider the hidden costs of all of your purchasing decisions. A car costs far more than the cost of the vehicle. You must include in the price what the ultimate cost of repairs could be over the next five to ten years, or the length of time that you plan on using the car. The same goes for any purchase, no matter how big or small. The cost of a powerful computer must also include the high cost of electricity for the usage of the machine. The cost of a house must include the insurance and maintenance costs over time. You can plan out the costs of these items by looking at either reliability for cars or the cost of usage based on the utilities in your area. It can be really difficult to combine these hidden costs with the sticker price of the good itself, but if you can do this, you end up with a much more accurate picture of what you can expect the total cost of any product to be.

CHAPTER 5: SMALL TALK

The Goal of Small Talk

In our fast moving corporate world, connections are part of the key to progressing in one's career. You need to make valuable connections with your colleagues, but you also need to network far outside of them, even simply within your company. These goals can be achieved, at least in part, through small talk. Small talk is the first step to forming a relationship with someone in your field. You need to be warm, friendly, kind and interesting, and all within a matter of a couple of minutes. The ultimate goal of small talk is to forge the initial connections that you will further develop in the future.

Knowing that the initial goal is to make a connection with another person, even if that connection is small and somewhat fleeting, the aim should be to find similarities and commonalities between yourself and those with whom you are conversing. Regardless of how the conversation starts, be it a topic of the weather or something more serious, you must always aim to try and connect with another person in some way. It can seem difficult to do this when dealing with such mundane topics like the weather, but it is merely an icebreaker to a more meaningful conversation. Remember that where a conversation ultimately takes you is going to be far different from how it starts. The types of connections that you make in small talk can then be used to connect on *LinkedIn*; and if you are successful in making a lasting impression, a connection on this social media website will be far stronger than the connections this person has made with others through small talk.

Topics to Start with and Where They Lead

Small talk by definition is not a long lasting and meaningful exercise. It is a conversation that only exists in the moment and then dissipates in the air just as quickly. The goal of small talk is to make a quick connection with someone and not to actually discuss topics that are of great importance. You will want to start with neutral topics when trying to start a conversation with someone; and when someone is starting to start a conversation with you, you will notice that they are merely aiming to engage in small talk. The topics that you can approach are far greater than those that are off limits. Feel free to discuss the setting where you are meeting, the weather, and other disposable and in the moment topics. I like to think about the categories of small talk that are approachable as subjects that are destined to change within twenty-four hours. For example, the weather is impermanent and the setting you are in is going to change. You will want to avoid topics that are politically charged or that bring with them a high sense of emotion and weight.

The topic you start with is merely a way to introduce yourself to another person. It is merely a way to get to know another person in a very informal way and to share the basic niceties of conversation. What comes next is where you start to make the longer lasting connections where you are essentially "networking." This is when you want to start getting into topics of work and the specific overlap that you and another person might have. It is during the early disposable topic when you want to express your humor and show the most signs of your personality. When you get to topics of work, you can start to be more serious and get into the details of exchanging information. In small talk, this second phase of getting into more detail and starting to relay information related to work is essential because this is the information you really need. To network on a professional level, you need to garner information about the other person's field. You need to be able to place them within the organization for which they are working and this only comes after you have had that initial established connection through talking about a disposable topic. When it comes to this second phase of conversation, there is one key piece of advice that will guide you: make your job interesting. When it comes to talking about our job responsibilities and our role within a company, we often get into the minutia or are merely do not descriptive enough. Instead, you want to focus on how you can explain your job and your role in the company in a quick way that is stylistically interesting. The best way to practice this is not all that different from doing a sales pitch: explain your role with the ultimate goal of making it as interesting as possible. Instead of the ultimate goal of making a sale to get the person interested in the product you are trying to sell, the ultimate goal here is to get the person you are engaging with to be interested in you.

For your part of listening to the conversation, your goal is to make the other person feel that they are fascinating. This might seem perverse in an odd way, like your lying to the other person about how interested you are; but it is a key tenet of how we engage others in conversation early on. You might need to feign interest at first if the topic is not captivating; but if you can get interested in what the other person is saying, you can make the topic much more interesting for the both of you. Focus on what the other person is trying to say and what makes their job interesting and you will find that you can get absorbed in their story. This can be a difficult step for many, but it is a key aspect of engaging others in fast and quick conversations. Not everyone you speak to is going to be fascinating, certainly when it comes to outlining the details of their jobs and their responsibilities, but you if you can make it interesting for yourself, you will be far better off and will have a stronger connection with the other person.

Breaking down the Two Types of People you will Engage in Small Talk

There are many types of people in this world, but when it comes down to small talk, there are essentially only two that you will engage with at a regular rate. They break down into groups of those who want to communicate and those who do not. Granted this is a very simplistic view, but it does show how small talk can either be easy or difficult, and rarely in between. There will be individuals who are delighted to have a conversation unrelated to work, or merely to strike up a conversation to form a quick connection with someone, and then there will be those who have no interest in small talk and merely wish to go on with their day. For the first of types two people, engaging in small talk merely comes down to the strategies mentioned above; you just need to get engaged and the conversation should proceed relatively easily. For the latter type of people, you need to take a slightly different approach.

Conversations with people who simply do not want to engage in small talk can be tough, but the key is to get as engaged as possible. It can certainly feel like pulling teeth at first; but if you can truly get interested in what they are trying to communicate, you will find that these types open up rather quickly. The real reason why certain people seem like they don't want to engage in small talk is because they feel that they are not good at it. Your job is therefore to reassure the other person. Once they have even the slightest bit of confidence that you are interested in what they have to say, you will see any disdain they have about small talk melt away. Think about it from your perspective; if you were poor at a particular activity, would you really want to participate in it? The moment this changes, however, you will notice that they suddenly do want to engage with you and do want to take part in a conversation. Make them feel comfortable and they will open up to you. You can then network accordingly and establish the ultimate goal of small talk, which is to build a connection.

CHAPTER 6: PRESENTING YOURSELF TO THE OFFICE

There are essential tips and strategies that can be invoked in any business setting. These are transferable skills that you must appreciate and learn if you aim to get ahead. This chapter will focus on these skills as they are applicable to all of your corporate goals. Even small achievements in body language and eye contact will help you get ahead and gain clout in your office. To explain this idea of why we need to make ourselves more masculine, to improve our status around the office, one must merely look to the Japanese and Korean languages and how their honorific system has formed and created their corporate culture, and yet is still an offshoot of the American business culture that rose to prominence following World War II. The idea here is that there are inherent advantages that certain individuals have in the office; in eastern cultures this is evident from the structure of their language; your goal is to emulate the strengths of the professionals at the highest positions of the corporate ladder.

There is a somewhat disturbing idea about what it means to make it in the corporate world in America. One must be willing to put themselves on a pedestal, to think of themselves highly. They must have the necessary self-esteem to be treated differently and rise through the ranks. This idea of special treatment for some is distasteful, but it is an inherent part of the human experience. For you and what you are trying to gain, you can benefit from how others are treated differently in an office setting. In western culture, there is a high correlation between height and attractiveness, and salary and position within a company. This is the distasteful idea to which I refer, but it can be used to our advantage. In eastern cultures that have an honorific system in their language, this discrepancy arises, too, but it is based on the social hierarchy given through job placement and age – attributes harder to modify.

In the Korean and Japanese cultures, your name is tied to a specific ending, tied to what your status is and your function at your place of employment. I mention this so that you can see the inherent advantage you have by working in any western office. These attributes are tied to the names of employees, their age and function. They are inseparable from the person and that is why job advancement in these countries is significantly halted in comparison to the United States and western countries. The point I am trying to make is that you can control how others view you; this is your competitive advantage. You can manipulate the way the office, your boss, and others see you by the way you move and act. Height is an inherent advantage in the workplace, and this does have the same type of discrepancy in pay in the same way that title and role has in Japan and Korea. These are much harder to separate and are forever tied to the employee; they simply cannot break away from this treatment.

Focus on the tips and general advice that I have in this chapter and know that you control your own standing in your company. Your work and experience matter, but there is more to your standing than just performance. It is also in the way you conduct yourself and how you treat and speak to others. If you can focus on these skills and improve the way that others see you, you will be poised to be in the best possible position in your company.

Self-Presentation

On the other hand, in several eastern cultures, employees must battle an uphill fight of working against the honorific system. The west has significantly more advantages in changing the way the world views them as a whole. The first of these is to improve the way you dress. This is an outward presentation of yourself, and one of the first things that others note about you. Note that this does not mean wearing extremely expensive clothing; rather, what I am talking about is making sure that you are presenting the clothing you do wear in the best possible light.

To ensure that you present yourself in the best possible way to get the type of respect and confidence you need, you must first look through your entire work wardrobe. This means going through every outfit and spreading them out over your bed. Take a moment and examine your clothing and ask yourself a simple question: "is this befitting who I want to be?" You must look forward to the future and your future self, and you must show the world that you are worthy of the attention you crave. Look through your clothes with this intent and remove the pieces of clothing from your wardrobe that you feel does not serve this purpose. This is the only costly measure I wish to provide in this book. I understand that this can be an expensive step, but it is well worth it in the end. The type of style you should be trying to emulate is not one that is general, but rather it needs to be specific to who you want to be. You are looking for clothing that is professional and clothing that you can wear well. You have within yourself the eye for choosing your own style, even if you don't necessary think you do. Just look through your clothing and replace the pieces that are out of date or fall out of place from the question you must ask yourself above.

The next part of your presentation is ensuring that the outfits you wear are in the best possible shape each and every day you wear them. If you wear a sports jacket to work, you need to make sure that every aspect of the shirt you are wearing underneath is immaculate. It is very easy to iron only the front of the shirt (something I see quite frequently); but you must iron everything, even what is not immediately visible. You cannot cut any corners here. You must also make sure that the clothing you put on fits you extremely well. If there is an article of clothing you quite like, but is a little too long in the pants or short in the shoulders, it is worth the cost of hemming the item so that you look your best in it.

Next you have your hair and hygiene to worry about. This is where there becomes a stark difference in what you want to accomplish depending on your gender. For males, I always suggest a clean-cut style. This is the most common type of styling you will see among executives, and therefore it is the style that you want to emulate. You can wear your hair long or give it a special type of styling depending on the market you serve. The tech sector is generally more accommodating of deviance from the norm, for example, but in general you are going to want to match what the people at the top of the ladder are doing. For females, I have some specific advice: clean but feminine. It is your style and your choice, but I would suggest not trimming your hair too short. You want to have the same character underneath, and I've seen more androgynous haircuts cause a bit of worry to many females' collogues. You, instead, should go with what is you, but make sure that your hair is not too long and that it is always well kempt. I advise against haircuts that are complicated, such as a perm, or styles that require a lot of maintenance or stand out as being overly unique. You want to be the model of confidence and that model has a predefined form.

Lastly, for this section I need to mention a little bit about culture heritage. The way we style and present ourselves to the world through our fashion and hygiene is partly based on our upbringing and cultural heritage. One cannot possibly ignore this fact, and neither should you. That being said, keep in mind what your ultimate goal in any office place is: you are trying to exhibit confidence. If you want to style your hair yourself in a way that is specific to your cultural origins, go for it, but always do so within the limits you feel are appropriate for your office. This does not necessary mean "white-washing" your appearance, but the truth is that those who want to stand out with cultural overtones shown in their hair and style will have a slightly harder time getting ahead. Trust me, it pains me to write this, but it is the truth of the world we live in. Don't abandon what makes you unique, but you will want not to stand out so much that you make others feel uncomfortable.

Body Language and Posture

Body language is perhaps the most important aspect of presenting yourself to the rest of the world. You must have the poise and manner of the position you want before you are able to gain it. This is a difficult skill to teach, but with diligence and practice, it can certainly be yours. You must merely know what to look for in your own behavior, style, and mannerisms, and work slowly to develop them to resemble the people in the position you want.

I mentioned earlier that there is a strong correlation between height and both salary and position within a company. It should therefore be no surprise that most of CEOs in America are taller than the average populace. This is not something you can change about yourself, but there is good news about this interesting aspect of human culture. I have found in my studies that it is not necessarily height that gives people an advantage, but rather that the height advantage has sparked what can only be described as a change in the way these people view themselves. They think of themselves differently because they have been treated differently, and their posture has changed over time. What you therefore need to focus on is your posture to mimic and imitate the type of skills that will garner you the respect and dignity so easily attained by the world's corporate leaders.

You have an idea of what good posture looks like; I have no doubt of this. You know that it requires you to keep your back straight, your arms outside of your jacket and holding your head high. How you can improve these skills is quite simple; you have to re-envision yourself as a person with power, a person who has the ability to climb to the top of the corporate world, and you will start to see the benefit of subliminally improving your posture. What I'm referring to is an old idea: the Law of Attraction. That is, if you can picture in your mind your goal, then you can train your body to obtain that goal from the mere desire of completing your objective. I do not believe that this can be used to make yourself win the lottery or start a romantic relationship with a famous actor, but what it can do is put in your mind's eye the things that you can control; namely your posture and stature in a room. You must want the changes you seek, and you must want to change the way you stand in a crowded room. Imagine yourself as standing tall, as being confident, and you will exhibit this confidence around others.

I understand how this idea can seem a bit obtuse, perhaps even a bit "new-agey," but I have found that this is the best possible way of achieving the strong posture and physical composition you need to truly get ahead. To demonstrate this, you must merely look at the most powerful people in the corporate world. It is not that they have focused on their posture and this is how they have improved how others view themselves, but rather it is the confidence they exude that led to their improved posture. You must therefore imagine this confidence, you as a confident person, and then you will gain the posture you desire.

The way to do this practically are to imagine yourself as the confident person you want to be, but also to practice a certain pose. If you are familiar with the pose that Superman makes on top of a building, if you can practice this posture, then you can gain greater self-confidence and improve your posture overall. As someone who touts the idea of the Law of Attraction, even I was skeptical about what this type of pose could really do to benefit someone; but as it turns out, there have been a number of studies that have confirmed this phenomenon. If you stand with your legs spread out, your arms at your sides, you will feel more confident. Perhaps you will feel a bit silly at first, but it has been shown that this will help the way you view yourself mentally. As such, you will improve your posture over time.

Eye Contact

Everyone says that eye contact is important, and it is, but what is often missed is the timing and where and when you want to make eye contact. To understand the importance and utility of it, you just have to know that eye contact does one thing above all other: it shows that someone is paying attention. The difficulty comes in forced eye contact and what this implies. Too much forced eye contact and the activity can come off as a farce, so there is a balancing act that needs to be made. Thankfully, this is quite an easy task once you know what to look for.

When you are disseminating information, it is important to have eye contact with those to whom you are talking. This can be very difficult for some as it increases their anxiety and heightens stress. Avoiding this is simple, just look at the nose for small encounters, and the forehead for encounters with a larger group of people. For example, let's say you are giving a small presentation to just three or four people. Aside from the time you are looking at your materials, you want to spend the entire time focusing on eye contact. This time should be evenly split between everyone in the room. In a small setting, you should look directly into the eyes or at the nose. What is important about this is that eye contact is a really good way of *forcing* someone to pay attention. By looking at someone, you are asking for their attention, and when they look back, you know that you are receiving it. For one-on-one meetings or smaller groups, you want to focus on eye contact as much as possible and follow the same technique. The most important time to look someone in the eye, or mimic this action by looking at the nose, is when you start to feel they are no longer paying attention, or if they are having difficulty understanding what you are trying to get across. By looking in the eyes of those you are trying to communicate with, you actually get those ideas across far better than if you are looking at some other part of their body, or the materials that you are trying to present.

For larger rooms, meaning rooms of ten or more people, you will want to focus on the audience as if they were a single entity. To do this, look at the forehead of audience members. In larger settings, it is much more difficult to ensure that the entire audience is paying attention. The best you can do is to follow the tips in Chapter Three to ensure that the presentation you are giving is as interesting and accessible as possible. Eye contact in this type of setting is simply a matter of looking across the audience as a whole and focusing on the individual foreheads of the audience members. You can certainly make direct eye contact with any individual member, but such action isn't actually necessary. For many, eye contact in a large room when giving a presentation actually increases anxiety, yet another reason to stick to the forehead method.

Preparing Yourself for Encounters

If there is one piece of advice you should take away from this book, it is that you must be prepared for the encounter you about to enter. The strategies and advice in this book have specific pieces of information for specific scenarios, but each requires the same level of preparedness. To illustrate this importance, think about when you are running late to a meeting or appointment. When you are about to be late, or the possibly of being late is open, that encounter becomes much more difficult. This is the same type of feeling you get when you are not completely prepared for the encounter you are going to enter. You must make sure that you are always ready and prepared, and you will do better in every scenario. This includes even casual events, like small talk. Have a game plan for every encounter and the experience will go over much more smoothly.

CONCLUSION

Thank you again for buying *How To Analyze People - Conversation Tactics: the Best Strategies for Successful Conversations and Negotiations for Beginners*.

You now have the essential knowledgebase you need to work your way through a variety of conversational settings. Whether you are trying to make a sale, an important purchasing decision, give a presentation, or just communicate in small talk, you have pointers that you can refer to make a lasting impression and communicate your ideas clearly and articulately. Remember that the guidance from Chapter Six can be combined with any of the lessons from preceding chapters to increase your success. You will need to go into every conversational setting with confidence to truly be yourself and form the lasting emotional connections you need.

As this book comes to a close and you start to invoke the strategies in this book, I want to impart one last word of advice: communication is the finest aspect of belonging in the corporate world. The business atmosphere can often feel metallic and lifeless, but it is through conversations with our colleagues and the people we meet through interviews and conferences that we bring a sense of humanity to our business as a whole. If you are ever worried or nervous in a conversation,

I want you to focus on this idea of communication as being the highlight of the business world. You should be proud to communicate with those around you, because this is the time when you get to bring humanity back into your career. Yes, you will need confidence to make a lasting impression and it can be daunting to go through any number of conversational settings when you are under pressure; but if you can focus on the appreciation that these human connections engender, you will think of these pressure situations as moments of relief from the rigid corporate structure we often find ourselves in.

Your next step is to get out there and start using the words of advice and strategies I offer. The goals that each of you will have are going to be very different from one another. This book serves a variety of purposes for conversation tactics in the business world, and you will need to invoke the right strategies for every particular situation you find yourself in. You have the knowledge; and with a little bit of practice, you will become a great achiever and form the strong emotional bonds you need to get ahead.

Lastly. if you enjoyed this book, it would be much appreciated if you could leave a review on Amazon. The best way for this book to make its way into the hands of more readers is through truthful reviews about the work. Please write what you liked about this book and what could be improved upon. Any and all feedback is helpful as I continue to serve the needs of my readership.

Thank you and good luck!

Free Preview: How Analyzing People Helps you

If you found this book helpful, you might also be interested in my other book How to Analyze People. In this free preview chapter, you will   learn how analyzing people can help you in different situations. You will quickly see how analyzing people is the perfect complementary skill to influencing people. How to Analyze People is now available on Amazon. Never stop to learn, never stop to improve! That's how you succeed and outperform your competition!

Although you may find this topic intriguing, you might wonder how this knowledge can be of practical use in your life. To put it simply, a whole new world of possibilities opens up to you when you learn how to read the behavior and feelings of others. Situations that once threw you into a confused state of mind with seemingly no way out will no longer be an issue for you. Dealing with "difficult" people will no longer be a source of stress and misinterpreting the wants and needs of others won't mystify you anymore.

Successful People are already Aware of this Power:

People who enjoy successful love lives, profitable money situations, and careers already know all about the life-changing and critical power of analyzing others confidently. However, this pursuit is not always so easy. For some of us, this is not an intuitive skill, and most people find that they have to study it quite intently to begin getting a grasp on the subject.

Anyone can Learn this Skill:

The great news here is that all people can learn the hacks, tricks, and skills needed for becoming great with reading and analyzing others. The incredible power behind seeing what a person is truly thinking can be gained by any person who discovers the secrets of analyzing others.

What are the Consequences of not Learning this?

- **Job Complications:** When you are unaware of how to read others, you are more likely to run into conflict at work. If you have ever wondered why your boss seems to have it in for you, or why you can't seem to make yourself clear to your co-workers, this information will help you immensely.

- **Personal Relation Problems:** Without knowing how to read your partner, a healthy and happy relationship is impossible. You will likely find that fights last a lot longer than they should, or that you simply don't know how to fix problems when they arise until you learn this valuable skill. Do you get into fights with your spouse and stop halfway through to realize that you don't know what you're fighting about or how to solve the problem? This can be helped by learning how to analyze others.

- **Trouble Understanding yourself:** True analysis of human behavior does not just entail reading others, but also knowing how to read ourselves. To be frank, without understanding yourself, life is going to be a struggle for you. And there is little to no hope of learning how to read other people if you haven't first figured out how to understand and read your own feelings and thoughts. Since this is a key factor in learning to analyze people, we will cover this in depth in the last chapter of the book.

The foundation of unlocking true connections with people, personal success, and real happiness is yours to take as soon as you become aware of some simple factors of body language and basic psychology. You can free yourself from the inherent limits of everyday communication by understanding the world in a deeper way. Don't allow yourself to be held back by your inability to read others.

How to Approach this Information:

Before you can gain benefits to knowing the information you are about to be given in this book, you need to know how to approach it correctly. Here are some considerations to keep in mind:

- **Use Observation plus Experience:** Although skills of observation are valuable and absolutely necessary when it comes to analyzing people, they won't be of much value to you unless you combine it with personal experience. This combination will aid you in learning to tell personalities and types of people apart from one another. It's impossible to take one single formula and apply it to every person or even their every trait.

- **Humans are Complex:** Knowing more than others about analysis of behavior will put you miles ahead of other people, but keep in mind that humans are complex beings. There is not a simple method for knowing everything about everyone, all the time. And any approach to learning more about this takes time and effort. Like any other skill, it takes patience and practice.

- **Interaction helps you Learn more:** Gaining conceptual knowledge through reading about a topic, for example, is helpful in learning about any given subject. But interacting with people is another great way to learn how to interpret them. This can involve eating with the person at a restaurant or simply going out for a walk. During this activity, you can keep a close eye on their mannerisms, how patient they are, as well as their general temperament.

Being in either a casual or professional situation with someone else will help you understand the way they function in various scenarios, along with how they normally act on a day to day basis. You can supplement this general observation with strategies about whether they prefer to work as a team or on their own, and to test their factual awareness.

- **Try not to Assume:** Although it's nice to learn how to read other people, it's important not to assume too much. Although you may get quite good at interpreting how others feel and the thoughts they think, it's always best to check for confirmation before you assume anything for sure. Look for multiple clues, including context and past behavior, in order to form a solid opinion and then try to test this by asking them for confirmation or observing their behavior to see if you were right.

It's about Knowledge, not Judgment:

Don't mistake the art of getting to know the thoughts and habits of others as a way of judging their character. Along the way, you will learn how to interpret other people, but don't allow other people to judge your willingness to learn or know. This is a good habit to form, one that can help you stay aware of the personality types constantly surrounding us in daily life. All people are ultimately different from one another; but by gaining understanding of them, we widen our perspective and abilities in general.

End of the free preview chapter.

If you are interested in learning more about how to analyze people, click the following link to check out the book on amazon:

Thank you!

Thank you for buying *How To Analyze People – Conversation Tactics*. If you enjoyed reading this book, then I'd like to ask you for a favor, **would you be kind enough to leave a review for this book on Amazon? It'd be greatly appreciated!**

All my best wishes,

Kevin Bradnik

www.ingramcontent.com/pod-product-compliance
Lightning Source LLC
Chambersburg PA
CBHW071814170526
45167CB00003B/1304